This
Particular
Earthly
Scene

This
Particular
Earthly
Scene

Margaret Lloyd

Alice James Books
Farmington, Maine

Acknowledgments

Grateful acknowledgment is made to the following journals
in which some of these poems appeared or will appear:
The Contemporary Review: "Law and Grace."
Green Mountain Review: "The Muse," "The Same River," "Preparing for
Winter," "Night Out." *The Minnesota Review:* "What Keeps Me Here,"
"What She Wants." *Passages North:* "Coming Down Rain From Light."
Planet: "Thinking About Playing the Violin." *Poem:* "What We Forgot,"
"What She Knows," "After You." *Poetry East:* "Backwards to Heaven,"
"The Letter." *Poetry Wales:* "The Simplest and the Hardest," "What My
Mouth Can Say." *Religious Humanism:* "Late Blessing."

10 9 8 7 6 5 4 3 2

Alice James Books are published by Alice James Poetry Cooperative,
Inc., an affiliate of the University of Maine at Farmington.

ALICE JAMES BOOKS
238 MAIN STREET
FARMINGTON, ME 04938
www.alicejamesbooks.org

Library of Congress Catalog Card Number 92-38198
ISBN 0-914086-99-5
Cover and text design by Charles Casey Martin

Alice James Books gratefully acknowledges support from the
Massachusetts Cultural Council, a state agency whose funds are
recommended by the Governor and appropriated by the State
Legislature, and from the University of Maine at Farmington and the
National Endowment for the Arts.

The printing of this book was supported by a grant from the
Frank M. Barnard Foundation.

Epigraph: H.D. *Collected Poems* 1919-1944.
© 1982 by The Estate of Hilda Doolittle. Reprinted by permission of
New Directions Pub. Corp.

Cover Art: Rodin, Auguste. *Fallen Caryatid Carrying Her Urn.*
The Metropolitan Museum of Art. Gift of Iris and
B. Gerald Cantor, 1985. (1985.56.1)

for John, Bryn, and Catrin

Contents

Satisfied, unsatisfied,
satiated or numb with hunger,

this is the eternal urge,
this is the despair, the desire to equilibrate

the eternal variant

—H.D., "The Flowering of the Rod"

I

The
Unquiet
Heart

The Muse

The statue did not lose her limbs and her classic shape
through accident or time but was fashioned

broken and dismembered by the artist.
She stands but she is asleep,

her head resting on her shoulder surrounded by bronze hair.
I admire her containment of unmistakable, large damage.

I am willing to dig into my own skin
if that is necessary for truth.

But my skin is not my skin.
My children breathe under it, wanting to grow.

In this house the erosions are small and daily.
There is little prayer.

What Keeps Me Here

What keeps me here is not
the light on leaves outside my window,

beautiful as I see it is,
or the thrumming of crickets

in the wet grass of late summer.
Not adult love, not the past.

But that flesh, that flesh
I put my arm across in bed

this morning, my small son
and the round face of my daughter.

I wonder how to make the birds
make a difference to me

as they wait in the branches.
How to raise my eyes from the sidewalk

I walk over, how to keep
my eyes off my own heart.

On his deathbed my father
asked my mother to let him go.

But I can't ask that of children.
All I can do is stay,

even if only my body stays
and I can't talk,

can't think about them.
Someone else plays with them,

sees to their needs.
But my body is here,

standing in a corner,
sitting on a couch,

walking abstractly in the garden.
Here to call to, here to see.

My daughter strokes my arm.
With each stroke I think

I am still giving birth.
Only my body can do this.

Sunday Afternoon

The sun is low, the woods darker now.
Nine bulls who were lying down
when I first arrived at this field
are standing. In town, my husband
and children move around our house.
They are beginning to think
of my voice, hair, skin. Anticipating
my return. They don't know
I have been staring all afternoon at bulls.
At one point the only movements
in the landscape were the mouths of bulls
and occasionally the flicking of a black ear.
They don't know this is what I left home for.

The Unquiet Heart

My son doesn't know I am gone.
That while I pour his morning milk,
I am wandering in a world where
everything keeps turning into something
else and I can't get back.
I am walking down an unfamiliar road.
When he sees me washing the dishes,
he doesn't know I am outside in a big city
at night, confused and looking for a signpost,
or walking up a country hill not able to see
above or through the tight hedgerows.
He sees me going out to gather kindling,
but doesn't know I snap the wood
until my palms hurt.

The Same River

Her son takes her breath away
as she watches him stand quietly

letting the cat move its long tail
around and around his thin, bare legs.

In this moment of pleasure which has nothing
to do with her, she thinks of a friend

who spoke of losing something easily
because he didn't value it

and then, upon recovery, finding it
precious. A game he said he plays.

She wanted to tell him, to tell
herself, this is dangerous.

We bring children down to the river to swim.
In the same river a man wades in waist deep

scattering his wife's ashes.
We don't see this man or know ashes

float in our mouth, catch in our hair.
All we know is the longing engendered

by each familiar portion of our lives.
A boy loving a cat,

a mandolin on a couch,
the wild apples of late summer.

Silent Body

She knew, the moment her body sliced the icy
lake in Goshen, the seven-week fetus was dead.
Her mother on the sand drinking tea,

her husband on the raft arms spread
about to dive. She turned on her back, let
water hold her silent body. Dread,

felt for three days with its constant threat,
became the certainty of absence: breasts
no longer sore, nausea gone, and her spirit

spent. Floating on her back she knew the rest:
the heartless cycle her body would complete
from the first string of mucus to a final nest

of blood in the water of the hospital's toilet.
The bitter relief that what the doctor called *tissue*,
and she called *life*, was gone. And the empty defeat.

Near the Shore

I like these rocks which change
every day with the sea.
Clear pools of water in reefs
with fish swimming in them.
The cormorant in the harbor
floating alone. I like
this rock which fits my foot
as I rest from the way
small rocks hurt.
My eyes enjoy looking
at the woman who spots two
wild black swans in the sea.
She can't take her eyes off them
as she walks along the pier.
Bryn finds a dark stone,
gives it to me,
and asks over and over
why I like it. I say
because it is round, smooth
with a perfect white circle
and he found it for me.
I like the way late afternoon
mountain shadows darken
the sea near the shore.
And knowing in this moment
that no one
with my blood is hurting.

Line of Yellow

for my father

I want to tell you now that my children
have painted land and sea you loved,

those sands you walked on, with a line
of yellow between the blue of the sea

and blue of the sky, so that sea and sky are always
separate, though constant in their blue.

One Christmas I was given two tea sets—
one a delicate bone china.

I played only with the common set
you gave me. I was loyal

in my sermons to neighborhood children
and my prayers at night.

Tonight I remember
that at the end you, too, faced

the complexity of inconstancy. David told me
on your deathbed you asked our mother for a kiss.

Her heart stretched one way and her body another.

Night Out

for John

I sit on the kitchen floor teaching my daughter
how to give a high five. She misses and hits me
in the eye just before I leave to eat dinner.
My eye aches all evening. Over Indian food
we discuss my latest project: nightly lists
of daily faults. Our friend, who once intended
to become a priest, talks about monks each night
writing down sins of the day. This information
really interests me. He says a monk might record
all the times he had not "custody" of his eyes,
the ways his curious, hungry eyes distract him
from thoughts of God, as he looks at a car going by,
a spider building a web, the patch of sun on his bed.
This list an attempt to tame eyes to do less.
My husband mentions a poem about a monk looking
at light and shadow on a page—"Pleasant to me
is the glittering of the sun today upon these
margins because it glitters so." And with a pang
I notice the way he wears his knowledge lightly,
his attention for small things. I think of that day
long ago when he walked down the street holding
the end of a long spider strand, watching it move
in the wind, keeping the thread aloft when wind
died down, watching sun make it appear
and disappear. There was nothing at the end
of that thread but everything, a high blue sky.

Lament

Sand, gulls, stunted trees
promise the sea—though I can't
yet hear the churning water.

The sea does not admire me
but I'm forever drawn
by its seduction. Playing
beyond reach of waves,
deep swimming in inconstancy.

The sea is not like God.
It is not like you.

Today I am afraid
I do not love the ways
we are growing old.

Stasis

Twice you watched while I was cut open
and a baby taken out.
Is it because you have looked inside me
that you now live
in the hardness of my bones?
In the bones which will last
after blood has spilled and dried,
my muscles withered.

All my life I've believed endurance is a virtue.
Every Sunday of my childhood
I rested in the words:
Lo, I am with you always,
even unto the end of the world.

I have a scar, barely visible now,
following the line where my pubic hair ends.
This is a secret you know well.
On earth, distance creates the possibility of desire.
I have walked along edges of this distance.
But I can't walk to, or away,
from what is inside my bones.

I Keep Walking Away From Home

I go down to the Mill River and listen
to water rushing away from me.
My skin, hidden all winter, desires
yet is afraid of the sun. More and more
living seems a matter of finding
the right distance so I can stay close.
I knew a man once who would rarely
sit across the table in a restaurant.
But sat right at my side, his hand
sometimes reaching down to caress
the soft leather of my boot in winter.

Inclination

Whether I leave home for a walk or three days,
my son kisses me on one cheek then the other,
waves from a window and signs "I love you"
as if I'm never coming back. Making me wonder
if I might not, might die, go mad, or fall in love.
Even the smallest things I do change me—journeys
I take only with my eyes take me away. I choose
one starling to watch swirling with a flock
over corn fields until it disappears in clouds
and I'm gone. At night I stand under streetlights
listening to crickets and locusts and I'm not the same.
A day like today is rare. I'm content with no desire,
happy to sit in the house listening to wind.
I want to watch my son's face as he learns to ride
his bike, be home to catch him in my arms.
Fra Filippo Lippi would give all he possessed
for any inclination he might have at the moment.
Today I'm glad I am not anywhere inclined.

Men on the Road

I'm driving to Springfield early in the morning
listening to Country 92.5—Dolly Parton singing
about a single yellow rose some man gave her.
I see a man walking along I-91, arms hanging
long down his sides. On the back of his brown
leather jacket in large white letters, GOD SAVE ME.
Maybe it's the long arms and the plea or the quick
love I feel for the truck driver who flashes his lights
to tell me it's OK. Maybe the music, but suddenly
I'm back in Rochester in a small practice room
listening to Maxwell play the piano for hours.
His long arms, fingers, long body improvising
only for me. Remembering the day we went
downtown to drink and landed in a second hand
shoe store looking for leather lace-up boots,
Maxwell holding up his long foot, asking
if they possibly had a boot to fit "this foot."
Which of course they didn't.

Preparing for Winter

If he were about to leave,
get angry, or die, I don't think
he'd be whistling as he walks
through the front door of our house.
And so something in me relaxes.
There is still time.

Our children find it easy to draw
what they have never seen. It is
their kind of prayer that I am lost to.
I'm like the geese I see in a cold sky,
leading with their heads and necks,
pulling heavy bodies behind them.

Still Life

I pick up the most nearly alive
of all the objects students have put
on the table, a pine branch,
and so the scent of pine is on my hand.
While students write I smell my skin.
I could wash it off, I think,
or let the odor of my body
gradually supplant it. Last night
I read about a woman who lost
her senses of taste and smell
and along with that the reflex
for affection. She would look
at her husband and children
and think, these are the people I love,
yet feel nothing for them.
When her senses returned,
love also came back.
I am grateful for this scent of pine,
though it is already diminishing.
I breathe and think of that perfumed air
passing into my lungs—lungs
which enfold a tired heart.

Moment by Moment

Outside of St. James' Church my eyes are drawn
to the statue of Mary, her hands curved
in front of her body as if wanting to stop
the sphere of the dove flying to her.
Trying to arrest the moment before
everything gets accomplished as it has to.
The front of her foot bends over the rock
she stands on, helping me remember
she was made of flesh. Her cheeks, darkened
by weather in London, were warm in Nazareth.
Did she think about the son she held
and had to let go moment by moment?
How one hot day, resting on her bed,
she heard his young step outside the door
and drew a cover over her body,
away from his sight for the first time.

Backwards to Heaven

Every day I teach my children what to want
while everything tells me my own desire
is too large, like the black bird in the park
which was bigger than my daughter's head.
In London last summer, I walked around and around
an image of the Prodigal Son naked on his knees.
Not bent in prayer but stretching his body backwards
to heaven. Praising not only his welcome home
but the world that kindled his desire.

What She Wants

For days after she is asked "What do you want?"
asked in such a way she has to think about it,
she forces herself to notice people wanting.
She stands for a long time at the salt marsh
watching a woman wanting a blue heron
to fly closer. Soon she notices that she too
wants to see the bird's large plumage,
that particular blue. And she is willing
to stand out in the cold wind for a long time
waiting on the bird's inclination.

That evening she watches her sister-in-law
wanting many things at once—to scrape the image
of a fish on stone, watch a movie, keep company—
and so she scrapes and watches, scrapes, talks
and watches. It is hard to observe her own wanting
in her daily life, where what she needs most is time
for what she has to do. She gets so tired, she wants
nothing but to go to sleep. She eats so little,
when she comes home she wants only to eat.
It is good to want in these ways she thinks.
Something about the world makes sense. But she knows
there is a larger wanting and finds herself
disturbed by the disappearance of ordinary desire.
The pleasures of entertainment and conversation.

When her brother surprises her by asking
the same question, once again she is left dumb,
noticing the passage of time, her head empty.
But he waits long enough for her to remember the image
from *Cries and Whispers* that has haunted her for years.
A woman climbing into bed with a woman
who is dying, who is living in the territory of death.
Love gets in the bed with death.
Love puts her arms around death in a small space,
in a dark room. It is terrifying and absolute.
The wild breast of the blue heron against her own
white breast. And nothing can happen after that.

II

Pictures
No One
Will Take

Law and Grace

After my grandmother died, no one was allowed
to drink from the cup in which he brought her tea
every morning or sit in her chair near the fire.
I was forbidden to play cards on the cold floor
of the front parlour where her body had been laid out.
I remember endlessly rolling clay
between my small fingers to make flowers
for the Garden of Eden while thinking of the paralysis
which had begun in her throat, her total silence
for two years before her death.

Years later, I believed when I heard a poet say
angers are not fatal angers, that silence is fatal.
I now know words as well as silences destroy and redeem.
Every day there is the possibility of confession or denial.
I yearn to have no choice—involuntary sounds of love-making,
inevitability of water rushing out of a bucket
turned upside down. I have never been able to live
under the law and I can't tell when I live under grace.

I do know that when I lived along the sea,
sometimes the sun went down so quickly,
if I turned my back I could miss it. Its being gone
was as final as anything could be.

Story

1

It is a chance meeting
on public ground. Polite
conversation is possible.
Only a backward glance
over a shoulder suggests
a future but no idea
they will walk around
for miles inside each other.

2

Having nothing,
they possess all things:
streets of the town,
a patch of grass,
whatever they choose
to look at, the common moon,
air they breathe, the inside
of a private note.

3

Not talking, she hears
the sound of words together:
You are my family.
No one has loved me
better than you. You
leave part of yourself
with me. I will see you
tomorrow.

4

But there is food to be bought,
children to care for.
Roofs are important,
familiar sounds in the night.
Paintings on a wall,
vegetables in a garden.
They are careful of everything,
careful for nothing.

The Simplest and the Hardest

I prepare for you the way I plan
for yearly visits from my brother's son—
deaf from birth, now a man.

I take the *Joy of Signing* down,
drive left hand on the wheel, name
with fingers of my right: *mountain,*

hawk, grass, cattail, flock, rain,
the world I see along the road. Words
unused, the way we never talk of *shame,*

regret. I sign and mouth the names of birds
for practice, recall and challenge limits
of my skill with him. We'll strain, beleaguered

by what we cannot say. And I admit
exaggeration replaces subtlety.
V's, signed with both hands moving, exploit

the complex truth, when all is *very, very....*
But something does come through. I make a fist,
draw a circle on my breast for *sorry,*

feel my beating heart. Sounds I resist
come from his yearning throat. The voice of a man
who has never heard a human voice insists—

shocking, strange, reminding me that human
voices are only imitations of sounds
heard from birth. I know the more I strain

to read the signs, the less I understand
both the simplest facts we have to learn
and the hardest. Like the relief of hands

allowed to be still as well as the heart
which closes and opens when he departs.

The Letter

One night I said we needed a bed.
You asked me if I meant
the kind you pay for. Sometimes
I would say things just to hear
the style of your response.
I wasn't at all interested in beds.
Why have a bed when we have earth,
a warm car, pine needles,
a bench, the sound of water?
You carried me down the bike path
kissing me and we were
completely held by the night.
Nothing in nature ever forced us apart.
For a long time the only person who knew
I loved you was someone who found
the letter I left between two trees
bending over the river.
Panicked, I returned and found it
opened, refolded, and replaced.
I looked up and saw a man fishing.
He threw his line out like a whip
and did not look at me.

Pictures No One Will Take

Last June near the river you cried
so long with your head in my lap
that my back ached and my neck hurt
from bending over you. But I would not move.
You told me of a man who shifted things
senselessly around in the woods.
Rocks from place to place,
leaves, piles of earth, and single
treasures. A nest, a bright button.
You said you felt like that man.
When you wanted to give me something in return,
I could not talk, but what I took was that man
who still moves wet stones
with early morning light touching and not
touching his hair. Slowly carries branches
to lie near a river the last thing at night.

Coming Down Rain From Light

My friend tells me she does not know
why she has a body anymore

and of course she is talking about
not being loved. I don't know what to say

but think of two poems
my daughter wrote last month.

One called "Coming Down Rain from Light"
about our roof leaking through a light socket.

The other, she said, was private
and I had to go into the next room

to hear her poem about rejection.
Even at four she has learned to hide

how she does not feel loved.
I think of a day years ago

when I sat in a seminar
smelling of semen, enjoying

the display that allows
people to imagine

I have been touched, my voice
heard, my body entered,

that perhaps I am loved
but at the least, I have been desired.

I love my children,
I hug them. In the dark

I put my mouth
on the neck of a man I love.

I don't care if God passionately pursues me.
If I have a body, I want another body.

Sweat, semen, the juices of our mouths
are rain from light

and I can find no words of comfort
for my friend today.

Theater

I listen to the myths that hold together
the life of a man I love. Myths
I have to face completely because they are
what will always come between us.
People hold on to old stories more than the truth.
I think, so this is the way love is dismantled.
For I am seen only if I can play a small part
someone else played long ago.

A part like the part of the woman who could not cease
kissing Christ's feet and washed them later
with tears, drying them with her hair.
Only a few words were spoken to her
and she was told to go in peace.
For those on that stage and for those who watched,
she played the sinner forgiven.

No one knows she leaves the house and idly
picks lavender from the side of the dusty road,
crushes it and puts it in her pocket.
That she has a child she loves. They laugh together
as they swim and float in the Sea of Galilee.
In two years she will die and while in this world
she was passed over, except as a theater
in which men's anguish lived and released
for a brief moment. No one pauses to wonder,
after she leaves the stage, how will she live her life?

First Day

This is the first day we will never be
in the same town again. I wake from a dream
in which you say goodbye to everyone
but not to me because of what you are
trying to forget. My head aches.
I walk to the bakery with my children,
holding myself as if you might suddenly see me.
I wonder how can I live in the eyes
of someone who is looking at something else?
Today I comfort myself by thinking
that everything I took, I used.
Even your weak eyes, which are now probably
bent on a grey road in front of you,
I use to straighten my body, notice a light breeze.

Stay With Me, Make Me Still

In the morning, with her hands on my cheeks,
my daughter tells me how beautiful I am.
She hasn't noticed my soul is gone.
In the afternoon I almost feel it,
confused and lost in the wind
beyond the maples outside my house.

My body bruises easily as if something
is trying to get in or get out. It is terrible
not to know, and not to know who will love
my children while my soul is gone.

Listening to Crickets

I remember wet grass and the man
who tied a white dog to his foot and lay
on my body to kiss me near the Mill River.
Odors and colors are released
only when the flesh is broken.
There is not yet a color I can name
for the way rocks shine when water runs over them.

Wanting and Not Wanting

I kept wanting to show him my scars,
all the imperfections of my body—
where my children were cut out of me,
the loose muscles of my stomach—
before showing shoulders, breasts, legs.
Not wanting to hide anything in the night
or in the exploration of what is inside
the body, the dark acres of heaven.
But I never did. And even now, I play
this communion of showing and looking
in my head, as if our mistake was not wanting
relief from seduction or the necessity of beauty.

Betrayal

The moon hung full, low and red,
huge in the not yet dark.
And I had to drive straight towards it.
When it shifted to my right I was
released. But tonight it is high and cold
in a black sky, broken in pieces
by the branches of a pine tree,
looking like the puzzle it is.
I have talked with many men
about the moon but I was
astonished by one who told me
he no longer thought of desire
when he looked at the moon. Later,
he confessed he had been lying.
But it has since then hung in the sky
like a question, like a blessing
that has not been reserved for me.

Another State

Once we lived across the cemetery from each other.
I can see it when I look out any south window.
His view was blocked by trees and houses.
After the first night when he touched my green cloak
and could not stop shaking, he spent hours
crying and looking at the graves of children.

Graves were always between us.
One summer, both out walking separately,
we waved and shouted, met at the corner
and walked down the hill along the cornfields.
He said that the day was just the kind of day
for calling across graves to someone you love.
At another time he confessed his favorite lines
of poetry were those about the grass
being the beautiful uncut hair of graves.

After our love was discovered, I visited
with my family another state. Early every morning,
left husband and children sleeping, walked
through wet woods to a country cemetery
to look at three old marble gravestones—
two sisters and a brother. All dead before they lived
a year. Content, I settled in on the long grass.

The Moving World

I know you are afraid
I will touch a magpie's wing
and you will have to remember
the moving world sends messages.
Flowers I love
lying in a rushing stream in Wales,
alter the water which goes to the sea.
And it is the sea you will swim in.

I think of you when I look
at the graveyard across a narrow lane.
Slate stones lean backwards
from earth shifting over time.
I like the truth of old graveyards
where what is over is not neat
but messy as our lives—
strewn with wildflowers,
overgrown with yellow grass.

Fall: Early and Late

In this town there is hardly a bench,
a piece of land, a street, a corner
of my mind, an hour of sleep,
not suffused by the failure of love
which I now know more
than I knew the inside of his mouth.

When I walk in the fields this late fall,
I am not cheered by the extraordinary blue
of cornflowers or the terrible, constant
blooming of marigolds in garden after garden.
The crickets no longer make me think of sex
in their thrumming. As the nights grow cold,
their song is slower, weaker,
more hesitant. And I am glad.

What We Forgot

Something we learn early disposes us
to see signs in the physical world
telling us in the midst of finally
some peace or joy that no good
will come of it. And when we look
back and remember the dented car,
smashed sea shells, glasses which broke
after midnight on New Year's Eve,
we think to ourselves—Yes.
That year we were doomed.
We forgot the cucumber seeds
were especially fertile, we
did not get cold from standing
with bare feet in freezing grass,
the branch over the water
held our weight. We forgot
the light that is not sunlight or
moonlight. We forgot
the very darkness acted as our guide.

Retreat

In this place there is no one
to speak to me. No words
from another mind, only those
that come from what I see—
little islands of ice,
red is the color of this winter.
And the words of my thoughts—
deliverance, distance,
it is best to have only one prayer.
Here I can know it is as blasphemous
to ask for relief from pain
as it would be to ask
for Mt. Ascutney, the red sumac,
or the squirrels to disappear.
It is a blessing to come to this place
where the dark gets as dark
as it must be
inside my skin at night.

Long Distance

Thoreau says he has a right
to love his friend and I believe that too.
You talked over the phone as if a year
had not passed, as if you really did not
think I had cost you too much.
Even better than your urgency
was the quiet when I spoke as if my news
might have to satisfy a lifetime.
Though you talked of how we closed one eye,
I know a person who loves
is like the Indian bird that dips
its beak in a bowl of milk and water
and drinks only the milk.

Stay Until the Fight is Really Over

Tonight I noticed when my hands
approach the fire, they hurt
where they have already been burned.
Our bodies remember pain and recoil.
But I think our self is drawn
to what has hurt it, wanting
to reach a deeper layer
of what is serious within us.

After fighting each other all day,
at night the Irish warriors
sent their antagonists herbs,
healing ointments, words
of love. At dawn, sustained
and strengthened, they furiously
resumed the fight again.

Our best self, however agonized,
finds a way to stay
until the fight is really over.
Like the wrestling Jacob
who even after his thigh is broken,
will not let the angel go
until he gets a blessing.

Late Blessing

I could not look at my mother's disfigured hands,
but I could do for her what her hands refused.
Scrape the new potatoes, untangle strands

of hair, plant with my children the bruised
red geraniums on my father's grave.
My children played on the stone as if used

to such a place to play. Hanging with brave
defiant smiles over the grey granite,
balancing upside-down to trace the engraved

name—their own name—with clear delight,
the cross my daughter called a sword, and finally
his date of birth and death at fifty-eight.

I wanted them to think of the close body
that remains and show another kind
of respect or awe. I wanted them to see

his head, hands, feet. Know the compromised mind
which I had to let go without a final
struggle or blessing, anything to remind

me I was loved and forgiven then and still.
With spades, a watering can, and an empty basket
in our hands, we left the cemetery hill.

Thinking About Playing the Violin

Tonight a robin flies
across the front of my car

and I don't slow down.
I am thinking about playing

the violin and about loyalty.
Flattery and fear of adults

made it impossible
to say no when I was given

a rented violin. I was laughed at
carrying it home because it was so small

and I was so small. Whatever else
playing the violin meant,

from the beginning it meant
humiliation. The rooms

in which men taught me
were cramped and had no windows.

They smelled of dust and rosin.
My poor notes fell in late afternoons

on schools' deserted walls.
I practiced for years

what I could never master
and did not love.

I was loyal
because I had been chosen.

Tonight I keep moving and thinking
through the dark countryside,

which is all I now want
to require of myself.

After You

The brown mourning dove poking around
on my lawn had no significance beyond
itself for me yesterday. It was a bird
looking for food. I lay in bed last night
between two rains—one sharp, insistent
on the skylight—the other muted, penetrating
wooden houses and softening the earth.
Today the wind is high and contradictory,
flailing branches force sunlight to shift
rapidly on my walls. Rain and wind are
only weather that I have to live with.
At night, I enter the children's room
and kiss their round cheeks.
These are my children and I simply love them.
Now, nothing is more than itself. I live
trying to get used to this—the vernal equinox
when the day is equal to the night.

Return

When he comes back, he will come back
counting all the white life that grows in the woods:
indian pipes, hemlock berries, mushrooms,
the trunks of birch trees lying on the wet ground.

When he comes back, he will return
like an actor who has forgotten which play
he is in, and no one in the wings to whisper
words, and the audience waiting.

When he comes back, he will come back
painting yellow furiously over blue,
trying to forget it was the blue, showing here
and there, that gave the painting distinction.

When he comes back, he will come back
like a monk crossing himself in a hurry
before entering the Abbey, so fast that all
we see is his hand touching his right shoulder.

He will come back looking like a man
standing in a doorway, then walk the town
like a ghost, seeing lovers on a bench,
in the movies, lovers walking in the park.

When he comes back, he will come
hungry, staring at the moon,
trying to light candles in a wind
that has grown steadily for two years.

Days Will Pass, and Their Nights

My garden flourishes.
I have given away

old and ill-fitting clothes.
The children are baptised

and my head still aches.
A god goading me on—

beguiling and relentless
in the day and in the night.

And I am good at thinking that simply
breathing the same air,

looking at the same moon is enough.
To touch a shoulder is sufficient.

But sometimes I imagine
there is another god

who does not place anything
deliberately in my path,

has no interest in improvement
or mortification.

Does not even think of me.

The Places I Go To Find You Again

This morning I stole time,
left church early
with the taste of wine
in my mouth and drove
to the community gardens.
I watched a man
covering peas against
the frost, a woman carrying
her garden's debris into
dark woods, the day moon
still in the sky. I drove
further into the country
to pray. Not to convince
anyone to love me. For now,
this is the best I can do.

What My Mouth Can Say

I see the light on the bell-ringer's throat,
long and white. As he lifts his head to pray
I see what I am not supposed to see:

his cowled arms ready in a private dark
to pull the rope and let his body sway.
I see the light on the bell-ringer's throat

appearing, disappearing. I forsake
myself every night trying to deny
I see what I am not supposed to see.

His body lifts to pull the rope, his neck
curves back again. I cannot help but stay.
I see the light on the bell-ringer's throat

and I know it is God who makes me break
out in sweat on cold nights for all the ways
I see what I am not supposed to see.

The wilderness will not be one I make
but one He makes for me. Still on this day
I see the light on the bell-ringer's throat.

I hear the bells and there is much to take,
much to leave, always what my mouth can say:
I see the light on the bell-ringer's throat,
I see what I am not supposed to see.

What She Knows

It is life and death. Her seriousness drives her
out of the wooden cabin in Vermont to stand
in the violence of a wind forcing leaves to expose
their paler sides, lifting Iroquois Lake
in a multitude of waves toward heaven
like the bodies of lovers in fierce bliss.
Small bluets strain with their mouths
full of each unexpected and relentless breath.
But she knows there is a wind apart
from the way it moves the world.
On Pumlumon mountain in Wales
where there are no trees and the grass short
from the grazing of wild sheep, she had felt
the wind blow, and blow violently
in her exposure, her own long hair
over and beyond her face, coloring
the world a deep red.

This Particular Earthly Scene

And, of course, we will never be in a position
to walk around our completed lives like we can
a complicated, large sculpture and see
how one of us had an arm tied to her back,
or understand the tension in another's body
by a leg thrust between his legs. We will never
see that a woman stretched her torso upward
from her recumbent body with one leg doubled
painfully beneath her. Know which limbs
had free movement, which were hopelessly
interlocked, or why the body yielded, why it
struggled. Unless it were possible to walk around
the whole form of our lives, we can't see which eyes
had to meet and which were forced to look only
at another person's back or only at the heavens.
We will never move around this massive shape,
discover a missing limb, appreciate how another part
performs its function, notice where the light shone
and what was left completely in darkness. Perhaps
in the east we would see a woman with her hand
on a man's chest, in the west a son holding his mother
on his back while leaning into the front of her body
for support. All of us acting out our spirit's joy or
agony, defined only against this earth-stone we walk on.
We will never see how some bodies silently hovered—
not assigned a part in this particular earthly scene.

*I am very grateful to the following people for their encourage-
ment and help during preparation of this book: Doug Anderson,
John Bollard, Ted Deppe, Jim Finnegan, Susan Finnegan,
Jack Gilbert, Jeffrey Greene, Linda Gregg, Joan Larkin,
Gayle Lauradunn, Tim Liu, David Lloyd, Chuck Martin,
Jody Stewart, and Sharon White, as well as members, past
and present, of the Group 18 poetry workshop. I owe a
particular debt to Jack Gilbert for all I have learned from him
about poetry over the past few years. I also want to express
my deep appreciation for the important relationships which
make a life possible—close friends, and my original and
present family.*

Margaret Lloyd was born in Liverpool, England of Welsh
parents and grew up in a Welsh community in central
New York State. She received a Ph.D. from the University
of Leeds, England, and has published a book on William
Carlos Williams' poem *Paterson*. She teaches at Springfield
College and lives in Florence, Massachusetts with her
husband and two children.

Alice James Books has been publishing poetry since 1973. One of the few presses in the country that is run collectively, the cooperative selects manuscripts for publication, and the new authors become working members of the press. The poets are the publishers, participating in every aspect of book production, from design and editing to paste-up, from consultation with printers to distribution and marketing. The press was named for Alice James, sister of William and Henry, whose gift for writing was ignored and whose fine journal did not appear in print until after her death.

RECENT TITLES:
Jeffrey Greene, *To the Left of the Worshiper*
Alice Jones, *The Knot*
Nancy Lagomarsino, *The Secretary Parables*
Timothy Liu, *Vox Angelica*
Suzanne Matson, *Sea Level*
Cheryl Savageau, *Home Country*
Jean Valentine, *The River at Wolf*
David Williams, *Traveling Mercies*